THE
DIAMOND
AND THE
BOY

The Creation of Diamonds &
The Life of H. Tracy Hall

THE DIAMON

D AND THE BOY

The Creation of Diamonds &
The Life of H. Tracy Hall

Balzer + Bray is an imprint of HarperCollins Publishers.

Photograph on page 37 by Tracy Hall
Photograph on page 39 courtesy H. Tracy Hall Foundation
Photograph on page 40 by Charlotte Hall Weight

The Diamond and the Boy: The Creation of Diamonds & The Life of H. Tracy Hall
Text copyright © 2018 by Hannah Holt
Illustrations copyright © 2018 by Jay Fleck
ISBN 978-0-06-265903-3

The artist used pencil with color and texture added digitally to create the illustrations for this book.
Typography by Dana Fritts
18 19 20 21 22 SCP 10 9 8 7 6 5 4 3 2 1
❖
First Edition

A ROCK

named graphite,

A BOY
named Tracy,

small
gray
meager

down

down

down

in the earth
waiting centuries
   for the right time
   to shine.
Then one day . . .

small
ashen
meager
  down
  down
  down
by a creek, in a tent called home.
  Penny poor, curiosity rich.
He has so many questions:
How does a radio talk? What makes a locomotive run?
But the answers float away like wisps of train smoke.
Then one day . . .

HEAT
seeps through
the earth's mantle
where continents collide,
    making the rock
    bend
    sweat
    weep.

HEAT

blows through
the air vent at school
where he hides from bullies,
    making Tracy
    bend
    sweat
    weep.

But in the darkness,
the graphite remains.
It's not diamond,
not yet. . . .

In the darkness, Tracy wonders
and wanders up with the heat.
He's not leaving his secret maze,
not yet. . . .

PRESSURE

is a vise,
squeezing on all sides.
The more tightly the rock is bound,
the smaller it becomes.
The only way free
is up,

PRESSURE

is a vise
squeezing on all sides:
loneliness, hunger, cold.
Tracy ducks into the warm library
on his way home
and stumbles on a marvel:

words from books fill in the
missing answers to his questions.
They become a fortress of knowledge
  and a map of hope.
His red wagon creaks under
  a mountain of pages
  about nature. And then . . .

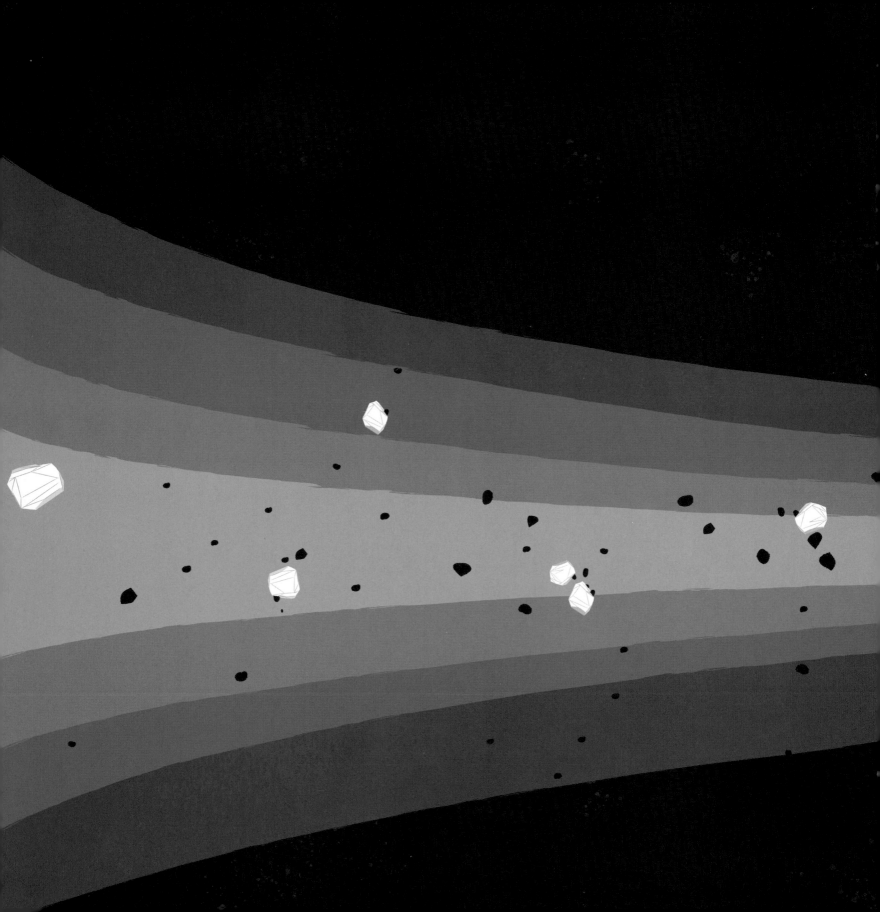

AN ERUPTION

shocks the ground—
a deep-earth volcano!
A rush of magma
runs hotter than hot.
The stone glows,
whirling as it is pushed

up

up

up

until the molten rock cools,
losing its strength
before reaching sunlight.
A glimmering vein of treasure
just below the surface.

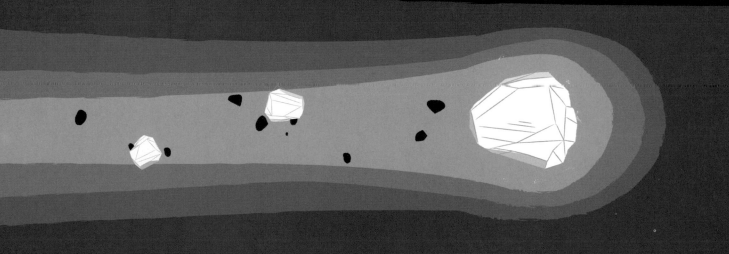

AN INTERRUPTION

ripples through schools across Utah—
a test! a test!
A rush of students bows heads to desks.
As Tracy reads the questions,
answers float

up

up

up

from books he's read—
one idea building on the next.
And the school officials
stare at this ragtag ten-year-old who
outscored all the twelfth graders.
A nobody—a skinny scrap of a boy—
with limitless potential . . .
just below the surface.

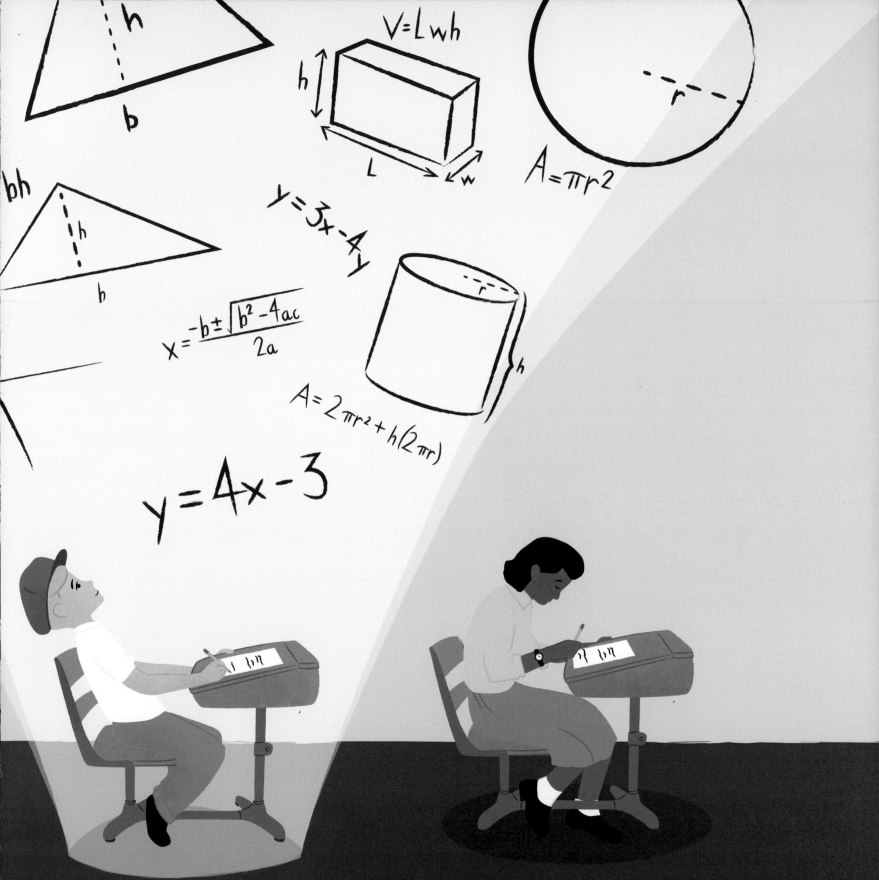

THE CHANGE
is clean and clear.
Crumbly, dull
graphite sheds
dusty clothes—
rebuilt from within.
Once fragile and frail,
it is now the strongest
crystal on earth.

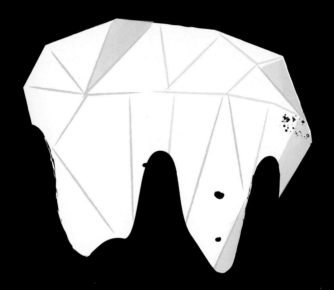

THE CHANGE

is clean and clear.
More and more, Tracy sees how to set
his ideas into motion.
A discarded pile of junk
becomes a go-kart.

Once-frail sticks and sheets
become strong enough to lift his feet
off the earth.

Mighty, unyielding, brilliant.
The rock would dazzle if it had
any light to reflect,
but it doesn't.
A crystal, even a priceless one,
is still only a lump
in the dirt
until it is found.

Mighty, unyielding, brilliant.
His inventions dazzle classmates.
But Tracy is still penny poor, with so
many ideas floating just out of reach.
So he cleans toilets before dawn to
afford college

and works late at jazz clubs for food.
Even a genius must eat and sleep
before his dreams can be found.

WAITING

to be discovered takes a small eternity.
Around the stone,
people search,
scrape, and fight for it.
The earth opens wide
like a hungry mouth.
A continent torn apart
by diamonds.

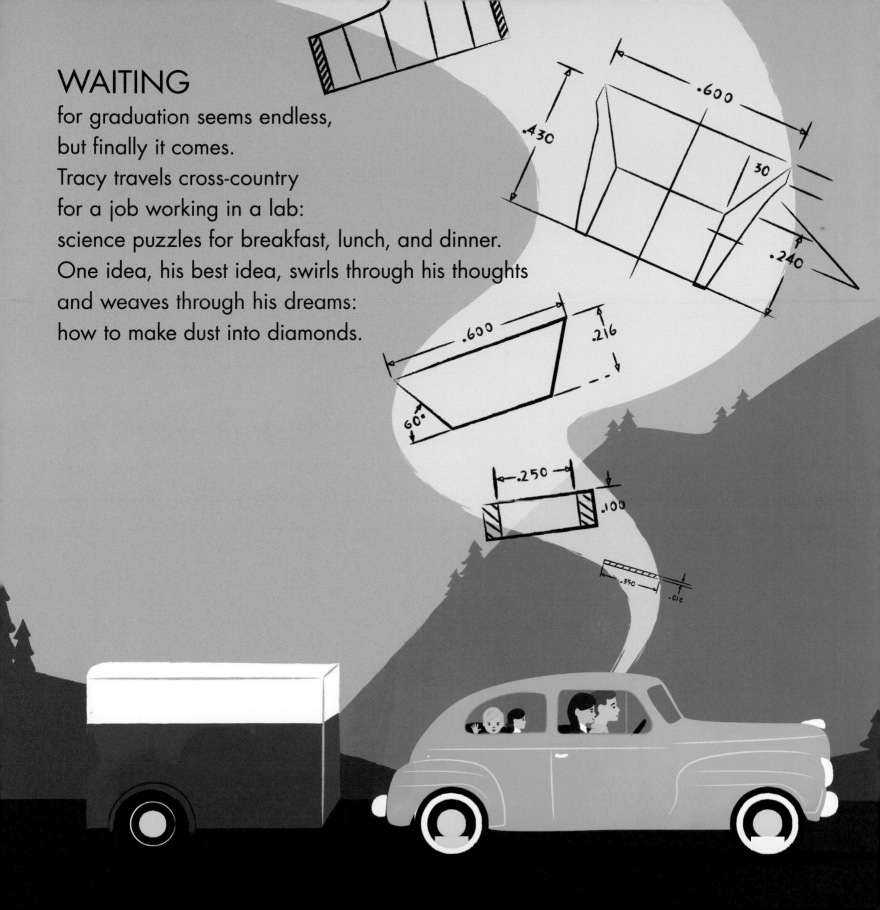

WAITING

for graduation seems endless,
but finally it comes.
Tracy travels cross-country
for a job working in a lab:
science puzzles for breakfast, lunch, and dinner.
One idea, his best idea, swirls through his thoughts
and weaves through his dreams:
how to make dust into diamonds.

Diggers come
and diggers go.
One thing's certain:
a
rock
is
patient.

But his boss won't pay for Tracy's parts.
His idea will never come to be. Unless . . .
In his spare time, he pieces
together his design from leftover
    machine parts.
One thing's certain:
Tracy
is
patient.

A drilling MACHINE
bores down in a circle, like a reverse
    volcano.
In dusty crevasses,
miners hunt for treasure
deep in the ground.
A warning horn blares. Then . . .

BOOM!

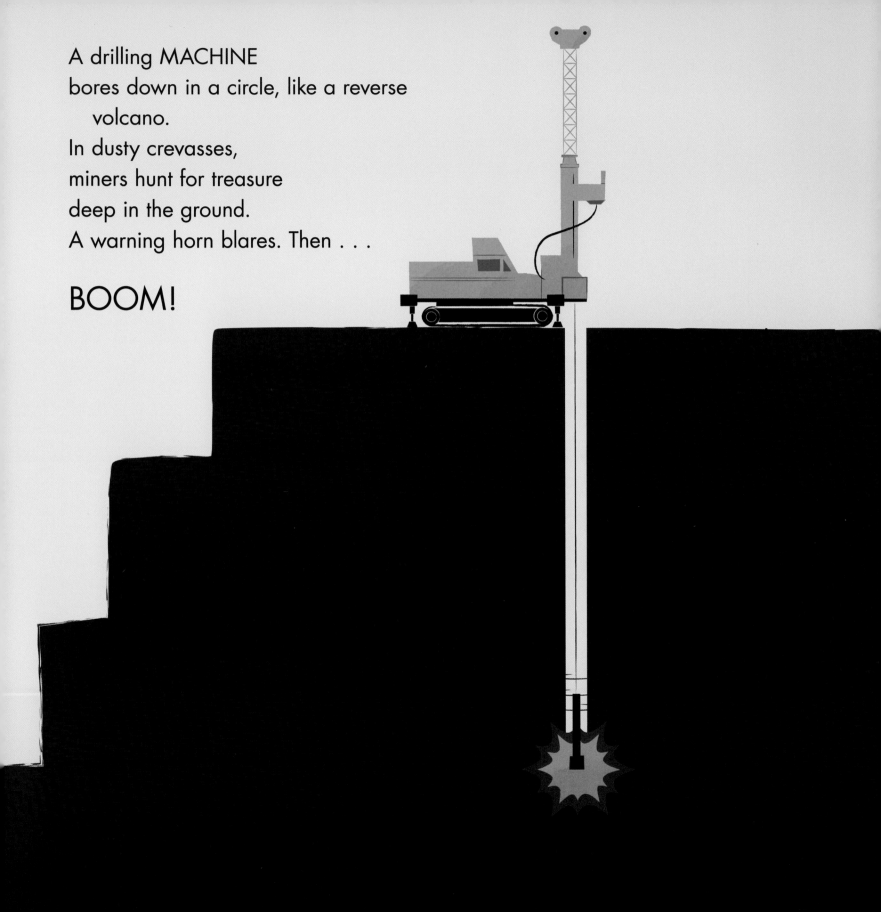

Tracy's MACHINE
is round and sloped like a volcano.
For his idea to work, Tracy needs the HEAT
and PRESSURE of a fierce ERUPTION.
Bang! Tracy ducks. Metal shatters.
Ears abuzz, he tries again.
Changes it. Tweaks it.
But nature doesn't like being bottled.

BOOM!

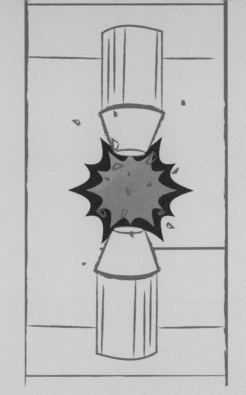

Explosives rip the earth.
Dirt goes flying. As a miner sifts
the troubled soil,
a glint
catches his eye.
It's small
    and gray
        but far from meager.
This rock is . . .

Stronger parts? More force? he wonders.
Then he remembers something he's read:
ribbons of iron surround natural diamonds.
Maybe the metal must touch graphite
for THE CHANGE to occur.
Tracy tries again. The WAITING is over.
The MACHINE doesn't crack.
Tracy's knees shake as he pulls out something small
   and ashen
      but far from meager.
This rock is . . .

DIAMOND.

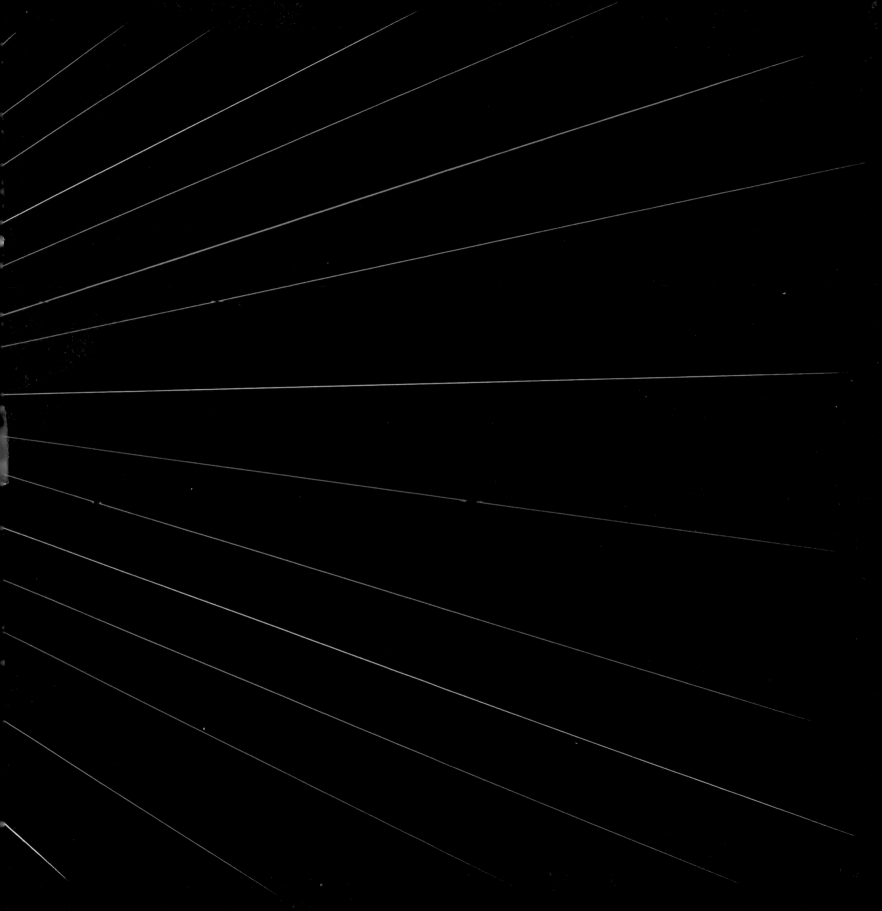

ON DIAMONDS AS GEMSTONES

In 1477, Archduke Maximilian of Austria gave Mary of Burgundy one of the first diamond engagement rings. Early diamonds came from riverbeds in India, and they were so rare that only the superrich could afford them.

However, in 1866, a child found an interesting-looking stone in a riverbed in South Africa. This neat rock turned out to be an over-twenty-carat diamond. Soon other diamonds were discovered nearby, and an African diamond rush began.

A flood of diamonds came onto the market, creating fear that these stones could become fairly cheap. A British businessman in southern Africa named Cecil Rhodes wanted to keep the value of diamonds high. He started buying diamond mines and eventually owned almost all of them under a company called De Beers. Since De Beers was pretty much the only company selling diamonds, the company could control the price.

In the 1940s, De Beers started marketing diamonds with the catchphrase "A diamond is forever." This further popularized diamonds as engagement rings, and demand for diamond jewelry soared. But the gem diamonds were sometimes hard to get, and many people stole and fought for them.

This struggle became a serious problem as diamond-exporting countries in Africa changed from European control to local rule. Unfortunately, some new rulers used tactics similar to those of their previous colonizers, including fear, forced labor, and/or neglect. This sparked rebellion.

In Angola, Sierra Leone, and Ivory Coast, local rebel fighters took control of diamond mines and sneaked the gems across borders. These rebels then sold diamonds to buy guns and bombs. Even elected governments sometimes used diamond money to buy war supplies.

Diamonds used to pay for war are called blood diamonds or conflict diamonds. Millions of people have lost family members, limbs, or their lives because of violence fueled by diamond money. In 2000, the United Nations worked to stop the selling of blood diamonds by creating a tracking system called the Kimberley Process.

The Kimberley Process follows natural diamonds from ground to sale with special checks and labels. The process was designed so that blood diamonds couldn't reach the open market. According to the United Nations, countries participating now represent 99.8 percent of the world's diamond trade. This means it's unlikely that someone buying a diamond today will accidentally help to pay for terrorism.

ON TRACY'S LIFE

Tracy Hall, 1932

In 1954, H. Tracy Hall (1919–2008) invented a diamond-making machine that rocked the world. His man-made diamonds were twins to natural diamonds but could be created in a lab in a matter of minutes. In contrast, natural diamonds can take millions of years to form.

At the time of Tracy's invention, the De Beers company controlled almost all the world's diamond supply, making diamonds expensive and sometimes difficult to buy. Yet only diamonds, the hardest material on earth, could do the precise cutting needed to shape everything from rocket ships to micro-chips, and in the twentieth century, manufacturing was booming. The world needed more diamonds! Tracy's invention suddenly opened a new way to get these super rocks. Today the roads we travel on, the cars we drive, and the gas we use are cut, polished, or drilled using diamonds.

For Tracy, making diamonds was always about the scientific challenge. Even as a child, Tracy dreamed of becoming an inventor, although life presented him with plenty of chances to give up. For a while, his home was a tent. At other times, he lived in houses he described as "dilapidated." It was the Great Depression, and his father couldn't find work. His mother served as a maid for a local hotel and stayed up until two a.m. every night washing and ironing for guests. But his parents always encouraged him, even letting Tracy saw, solder, and hammer his inventions on the kitchen table.

The family also helped care for Tracy's aging grandparents. Tracy's grandpa Hall had worked with the railroad. Trains fascinated Tracy, and he wanted his grandpa to tell him all about them. But on this subject his grandpa stayed silent (he was likely in the early stages of undiagnosed Alzheimer's). I know how Tracy felt because I too had a quiet grandpa—him.

Many times I sat with Grandpa Tracy, wanting to talk with him about his work and life. However, Tracy also developed Alzheimer's, and as the disease progressed, he gradually forgot everything, including my name. Through researching this biography, I finally met my grandfather and learned that he was funny and kind and passionately curious.

The rocks Tracy made in 1954 were small, colored diamonds, which were great for concrete sawing and other industrial uses. However, they weren't popular for jewelry. Creating large, clear, and colorless diamonds proved to be an ongoing challenge. So while lab-created diamonds have played a huge role in how we make and shape everyday items, it wasn't until more recently that they've entered the jewelry market.

A TRIAL OF FIRE

All diamonds—whether from the lab or the earth—go through a trial of fire. One of Tracy's favorite Thomas Edison quotes was "Genius is 1 percent inspiration, 99 percent perspiration." Tracy believed in the power of hard work and the idea that sometimes the most amazing discoveries are made on the twentieth or one hundred twentieth try. After all, it's persistence in the face of heat and pressure that transforms crumbly graphite into a stone of lasting beauty and strength.

A BRIEF HISTORY OF DIAMONDS AND TRACY HALL'S LEGACY

circa 400 B.C.   Diamonds are discovered in India.

327 B.C.   Alexander the Great brings the first diamonds to Europe from India.

A.D. 1477   Archduke Maximilian of Austria gives Mary of Burgundy the first diamond engagement ring.

1866   Fifteen-year-old Erasmus Jacobs finds the first diamond in South Africa, a large yellow stone later called the Eureka Diamond.

1871   The Kimberley Mine in South Africa is established, after the first discovery of an underground diamond vein there. (Prior to this, most diamonds were found by chance in riverbeds.)

1916   Diamond mining begins in Angola.

1919   Tracy Hall is born in Ogden, Utah.

1930   Diamonds are discovered in Sierra Leone.

1947   The De Beers company popularizes diamonds as a symbol of romantic love with the slogan "A diamond is forever." Diamond engagement ring sales soar.

1949   Tracy Hall begins work at General Electric.

1952   Tracy Hall designs his first diamond-making machine. It doesn't work.

1953   Tracy Hall designs his second diamond-making machine. It might work, but initially he doesn't have access to the right parts.

1954   Tracy Hall finishes his machine and makes a breakthrough with diamonds in the lab!

1955   Large diamond deposits are discovered in Russia.

1957   General Electric begins commercial diamond production. Meanwhile, Tracy Hall improves the process with a new diamond-making apparatus called the tetrahedral press.

1959   Synthetic diamonds make up 10 percent of the world's industrial diamond supply.

1968   Tracy Hall further improves the diamond-making process with a new press, the cubic press.

1975–2002   Angola is embroiled in a civil war, with diamonds used to finance the fighting. Human rights violations are rampant.

1980   Tracy Hall receives Man of the Year Award from the Abrasive Engineering Society.

1981	Tracy Hall retires.
1991–2002	Civil war breaks out in Sierra Leone. Rebel fighters drive civilians out of diamond-rich areas and use diamonds to fund a war against the elected government. Civilians are often targets of rebel attacks.
1998	Diamond mining begins in Canada.
2000	The United Nations introduces the Kimberley Process Certification Scheme for tracking diamonds.
2002–2007	The Republic of Côte d'Ivoire experiences civil war. Diamonds help fund fighting.
2003	The Kimberley Process is fully implemented.
2008	Tracy Hall passes away at his home in Provo, Utah.
2010	Tracy Hall is inducted into the National Inventors Hall of Fame.
2010–11	The Republic of Côte d'Ivoire endures a second civil war. Again, diamonds become a funding tool.
2015	Man-made diamonds make up 99 percent of the world's industrial diamond supply and 1 percent of the diamond gem market.

Tracy Hall with an early man-made diamond, 1955

Tracy Hall with the author, 1983

SELECTED BIBLIOGRAPHY

Cleveland, Todd. *Stones of Contention: A History of Africa's Diamonds*. Athens, Ohio: Ohio University Press, 2014.

Hall, Tracy. *1933–1935 Journal*. Ogden, Utah.

——. Transcript of tape recording: "The Diamond Discovery." 1964.

Hazen, Robert M. *The New Alchemists: Breaking through the Barriers of High Pressure*. New York: Times Books, 1993.

Howard Tracy Hall. South Jordan, Utah: Legacy Books, 2012.

Kimberley Process. Accessed 25 July 2016. www.kimberleyprocess.com/en/about.

Lineberry, Cate. "Diamonds Unearthed." *Smithsonian* magazine, Dec. 2006. Accessed 25 July 2016. www.smithsonianmag.com/science-nature/diamonds-unearthed-141629226.

Sheehan, Sean, and Jui Lin Yong. *Angola*. New York: Marshall Cavendish Benchmark, 2010.

Sheehan, Patricia, and Jacqueline Ong. *Côte d'Ivoire*. New York, Marshall Cavendish Benchmark, 2010.